Soul Mending

Healing
into
Wholeness

Soul Mending

Healing into Wholeness

Rev. Julia Pferdehirt, M.A., LPC

soulmending.live

ISBN: 979-8-218-24961-8
Library of Congress Control Number (LCCN): 2023914195

2023 Edition
Self-published in San Francisco, CA, using lulu.com.

Book design by Michael Thomas Holmes, mtholmesdesign.com
Cover photography by Kelsey Evergreen, kelseyevergreen.com
Branch and leaf illustrations © Elements Kit via Creative Market

Permission requests: infosoulmending@gmail.com

This workbook is dedicated to women who've felt lost, paralyzed, not listened to, and of no worth.

I hear you and we are here for you.

Thanks for showing up. It will be worth your while.

—Julia

TABLE OF CONTENTS

SOUL MENDING: AN INTRODUCTION

Welcome, dear friends, to *Soul Mending: Healing into Wholeness*.

I have a simple question … Why are you here?

Let's help you with your answer: if you've suffered a great loss in your life … been physically or emotionally abused by someone you thought you could trust … still experience deep disappointment or regret over something in the past … perhaps you are disappointed with God … maybe you've been betrayed or rejected by a family member or friend … sometimes even seemingly small hurts can fester over the years, wounding our souls.

If so, you have come to the right place.

Soul Mending: Healing into Wholeness … A journey from hurt and trauma to the healing of our very souls.

These *Soul Mending* videos and written teaching and personal reflection materials are formatted to be used in group settings with a facilitator. However, they may also be used by individuals as a workbook to explore their own experiences and healing work. In large settings, small breakout groups are best suited to share about and discuss the topic and reflection questions for each session. Use the "Tips for Breakout Group Leaders" section to help facilitate small sub-groups.

TIPS FOR BREAKOUT GROUP LEADERS

Breakout Groups work best when the same members participate through all the sessions. Consistency in groups encourages connection and creates an atmosphere of trust and safety.

Group size

The large group might be anywhere from 10 to 50 participants.

- However, the larger the group, the more important it is to divide the group into smaller breakout groups for the primary discussion of that session's topic (after reading the initial text and/or viewing the first video for that session).

Breakout Group size

- Conventional wisdom says that the ideal "small group" size should be no more than 10-12 persons.

- However, for these sessions with a limited time for discussion of 35 minutes, keep in mind that "smaller is better."

- For instance, if you have a "large group" of 10-12 persons, consider two breakout groups of 5-6 persons (one of whom is a facilitator).

- If your large group is truly large (e.g. 30-50 persons), do your best to divide into breakout groups of between 5-10 persons.

- Breakout groups can pull their chairs into smaller circles in the "large room" or go to smaller classrooms if they are easily accessible and don't take too long to "go to" or "come back from."

Breakout Group leaders should

- Interrupt "cross talk." Suggested language includes no advice-giving or fixing, please.

- Avoid using scripture even if you believe it might be encouraging. Remember, just because you find scripture particularly helpful, it doesn't mean other people will.

- Encourage active listening. Examples could include nodding, saying "yes," or "that was helpful to me," or "thank you."

OTHER TIPS FOR FACILITATORS

Large Group Reflection Guidelines

- *Model* sharing personal insights or experiences only, please.

- Reminder: no cross talk! (We cannot remind people enough.) Advice giving and fixing can interfere with what God is already actively doing.

Danger to self and others

- Request consent for emergency contact information at the beginning of the program.

  If any group participants talk about harming themselves or others, please:

  - Call 911 and request a well-being check, if concerned.

  - Do not assume self-harm, and/or that an individual is cared for by a mental health professional.

Closing group with announcements

- Closing Immanuel Prayer is included on each session's concluding video.

- Close with any information needed for the next session— including a reminder to read the printed text and answer the Reflection Questions for the next session.

Overview of each session

- A welcome and any housekeeping information presented by a group leader on-site or via video conferencing.

- A video by *Soul Mending* creator, Rev. Julia Pferdehirt, M.A., LPC., summarizing the session topic.

- Breakout groups.

- A 10-minute, large-group sharing.

- A concluding video, introducing the next session topic and ending with an Immanuel Prayer moment— bringing the work, emotions, and insights of that session to Jesus for insight and healing.

The videos for Soul Mending: Healing into Wholeness *can be found online at:*

soulmending.live

Viewing order has been indicated within the text of this workbook.

Suggested Schedule

For a 90 (or 100) minute Workshop Session

NOTE: Participants should read the upcoming session's printed text/teaching and answer the Reflection Questions prior to attending the group session.

Welcome (5 minutes).

Watch opening video: Summary of teaching for this session (10-15 minutes).
    Discuss Breakout Group guidelines.

Release participants to Breakout Groups (5 minutes). *
    *Video conferences or small settings without breakout groups will be 90 minutes, as they do not require this extra 10-minute transition, resulting in a 100-minute session schedule.

Breakout Groups (35 minutes).
    Printed group questions are found in the Session Workbook.

Break and return to Large Group (5 minutes).
    In settings where Breakout Groups are physically spread out in a building, 10 minutes may be required to allow for transition and restroom/coffee/water breaks.

Breakout Group reflections in large group (10 minutes).
    Significant insights? Personal or shared breakthrough? What's happening in your group this week? See "Tips for Breakout Group Leaders" section for Group Reflection Guidelines.

Watch concluding video: Wrap up and introduce topic and material for next session (15 minutes).

Closing Immanuel encounter (5 minutes).

Facilitator closes session with any announcements.
    Remind participants to read the printed text/teaching at the beginning of the next session and answer the Reflection Questions *prior* to coming to the group.
    See "Tips for Breakout Group Leaders" section for additional notes and suggestions.

Welcome to Soul Mending.
I'm glad you're here.

Please watch the video entitled "Introduction".

This and all other videos can be found online at soulmending.live.

Be Real.

Feel.

Deal.

Heal.

SESSION ONE

HURT, HARM, AND IMPACT

In the week before Session ONE, read the following and respond to the Reflection Questions for Thinking and Journaling.

Participants may also want to review the Breakout Group suggestions prior to participating in Session ONE.

Session One
Hurt, Harm, and Impact

When humans are **hurt,** we often feel angry or sad. These are "presenting" emotions— the feelings that jump into our awareness quickly. Underneath these emotions are deeper feelings like betrayal, fear, abandonment, powerlessness, shame, pain, or loss.

Hurt is real. Often, because it seems minor or doesn't result in intense or lasting pain, we dismiss or minimize it. We think, "Oh my feelings were hurt," and tell ourselves, "Don't make a big deal about it," or, "Let it go."

Hurt might look like disappointment. Someone lets us down or fails us. Someone we trusted betrayed that trust. Something we hoped for is denied, and we feel let down or ignored.

Hurt is felt *inside*. It can cause us to withdraw, to become self-protective. And, hurt is also "entry level."

Repeated experiences of hurt become **harm.** Harm results in damage and loss to us or to those we care about. Harm can break us, keeping us from living as whole people.

Harm is felt inside as emotion, and harm is experienced outside as hindrance, confusion, and damage to our relationships, worldview, capacity for awareness or action, and ability to choose to take the actions needed to live the way we want to live.

We are **hurt.** We experience disappointment, betrayal of trust, being ignored or treated with disrespect,unkindness, or even cruelty. Those experiences— and the emotions they elicit— pile on top of each other to **harm** us. Those "inside" experiences may become "outside" experiences. For example, disappointment and betrayal of trust may lead us to avoid commitment or to run at the first sign of difficulty. We might move from job to job or relationship to relationship— always fearing the next betrayal.

Harm is when we have been damaged by an experience. We have lost something that safe, unharmed people are supposed to have.

Intense or repeated hurt increases **impact**. Our sense of identity and worth is damaged. Our ability to function in relationships and in life is damaged. Damage leads to loss.

What loss? Loss of trust. Loss of ability to feel safe in life or relationships. Loss of self-confidence or ability to make decisions without doubt and fear. Loss of a capacity to feel joy.

Chronic disappointment can damage our ability to stick with tasks and keep us in cycles of hopelessness and giving up. When our self-worth is damaged, we may believe we are not deserving of love and relationship. We may believe failure and loss are simply the way things are.

Then, we lose the resilience that gets us through difficult times. With each perceived failure, we begin to believe we are failures. The pile of hurts and harm gets higher. The losses get greater— lost hope, lost belief that our dreams matter, that we matter, that our lives matter.

The impacts of hurt and harm— damage and loss— can be very, very practical. Loss is not just a feeling of confusion or lack of direction; it looks like something. It has a tangible impact, such as:

- Autoimmune deficiencies (migraines, chronic fatigue syndrome, fibromyalgia, psoriasis, Crohn's disease, arthritis)

- Insomnia

- Anxiety (worry, fear, panic)

- Hypervigilance (always watching, always aware and feeling afraid, nothing feels safe, no place feels safe)

- Fear of risk-taking, or taking repeated, dangerous risks

- Difficulty sustaining relationships, fear of commitment

- Difficulty keeping a job

- Difficulty finishing what one starts

- Difficulty setting personal boundaries (rarely saying, "No," letting people in too easily and without evidence they are actually trustworthy, not knowing how to protect oneself)

- Setting so many boundaries that no one can get close

- Difficulty trusting anyone, regardless of evidence of trustworthiness

- People-pleasing (agreeing with others to avoid conflict, being generally submissive in relationships)

- Anger/fight responses ("I feel like the top of my head blows off"), or leaving (slamming the door behind oneself, whether in reality or figuratively)

- Insecure decision making (second-guessing, inconsistency, being afraid to decide, not trusting one's own judgment)

- Intense, sometimes overwhelming feelings

- Numbness (not feeling much at all, feeling disconnected from life, others, or relationships)

- Fear of failure ("don't even start, you'll just fail," pulling back at the first sign of difficulty)

As you read this list, feel free to add other ways you experience the impacts of hurt and harm in real life situations. On the list, note any impacts you have personally experienced with a star, and note any you have observed in other people with a check mark.

Please complete the Reflection Questions in preparation for Session ONE.

Please use this space for your reflections and responses.

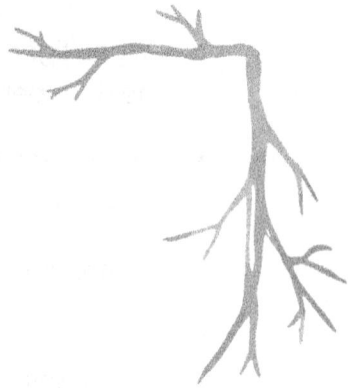

REFLECTION QUESTIONS
FOR THINKING AND JOURNALING

Reflecting on hurt, harm, and impacts, write any thoughts or memories of:

- An experience where you were hurt

- An experience when multiple or severe hurts resulted in harm

- An experience where you now recognize any of the impacts listed above

Choose one experience. Think and write about the following questions:

- What happened?

- How did/do I feel about that?

- What impact/effect(s) did this experience have on me "inside?"

- What impact(s) did this experience have "outside" in practical, real-life ways?

- What would I like to happen now?

Finally, spend some time with God.

- Rest

- Let yourself be quiet

- Listen

- Breathe

Ask God, "Please show me an experience where I was hurt and harmed."

Write a little about that experience. You may use the questions above if it helps you explore this experience.

END of preparation for Session ONE.
Group session begins on the following page.

Please use this space for your reflections and responses.

WATCH VIDEO

Please watch:
Session ONE
Hurt, Harm, and Impact
at soulmending.live

BREAKOUT GROUPS

Facilitator: Please read these group guidelines at the beginning of this first session.

Welcome to this group and to the *Soul Mending* workshop. Here are some group guidelines:

Confidentiality: What is said in this group, stays in this group. Please do not share or disclose what occurs in your group to others, including partners, leaders, or close friends. Instead, please feel free to talk about your own feelings, thoughts, and experiences.

Exceptions to the expectation of confidentiality include your own disclosures to a therapist or mental health provider or the rare instance that an individual's words or behavior suggest they may be a danger to themselves or others. In that case, a professional should be contacted immediately. Please see "Tips for Breakout Group Leaders" for details.

If you speak about conversations in this group to a therapist, please do not disclose any identifying information about the group or participants. This is respecting both the confidentiality of this group and the people in it. Thank you.

No Cross Talk: This guideline for *Soul Mending* groups is taken from Twelve-Step Programs. "No cross talk" means each person shares their own experiences, thoughts, and feelings. Group members do not give advice, solutions, or directions to others. This includes "helpful" Bible verses and information about what worked for you or someone else. In short, no fixing. No advice.

When a group member shares their own experiences, thoughts, and feelings, a welcome and supportive response that is NOT fixing, advice-giving, or directive might be:

- "Thank you for saying that."

- "I appreciate your insight. That helps me."

- "Thank you for being [honest, vulnerable, so real]."

- "Thank you for sharing."

The desire to help is admirable, but the impulse to fix and give advice, while a common human behavior, is not helpful. Group facilitators will remind participants of the "no cross talk" guideline, if needed.

BREAKOUT GROUP QUESTIONS

Your group may choose to answer any, all, or none of these questions.

- Choose one question for everyone to answer
- Each person chooses their preferred question to answer
- Group members create their own question(s)

In short, your group gets to choose the focus of discussion and sharing.
Please stick with the topic that participants read in preparation for Session ONE and/or watched in the video– part of processing information or principles is exploring together in this group.

Suggested Questions:

Thinking about hurt and harm, did you have any insights or "aha" moments?

- What was the insight?
- What are your thoughts about it now?
- What are your feelings?

Describe one experience of hurt and harm that came to mind this week.

- What happened "to" me?
- What impact or effects did that experience have "in" me?
- How do I feel about that?

The list of impacts of hurt and harm is a long one. What emotional, relational, physical, financial, or other impacts do you see in your own life?
As you thought about hurt and harm you've experienced and the impacts in your life, what is your strongest emotion?

- What does that emotion look like/feel like when you experience it "inside?"
- What does that emotion look like if you let yourself express it?

Please use this space for your reflections and responses.

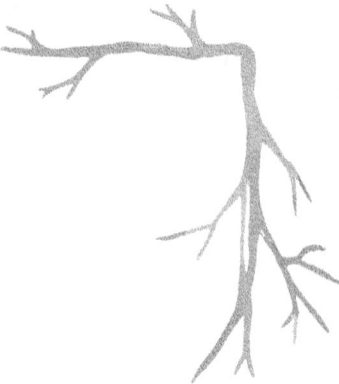

As you read about hurt, harm, and impacts, what memories came to mind?

- How do you feel about that?
- What thoughts do you have about those memories now?

LARGE GROUP

After breakout sessions, return to the large group. Spend 10 minutes sharing valuable insights from the Breakout Group.

WATCH VIDEO

Please watch:
Session ONE
Hurt, Harm, and Impact
Conclusion
at soulmending.live

15 minute teaching wrapping up this session, introducing the topic and preparations for the next session, and leading participants in Immanuel prayer.

Facilitator ends the session with any announcements.

Please use this space for your reflections and responses.

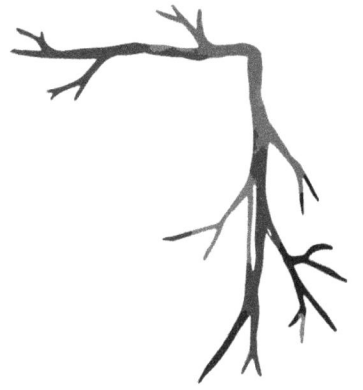

SESSION TWO

BROKEN HEARTS,
BROKEN PARTS

In the week between Sessions ONE and TWO, read the following and respond to the Reflection Questions for Thinking and Journaling.

Participants may also want to review the Breakout Group suggestions prior to participating in Session TWO.

Session Two
Broken Hearts, Broken Parts

God sees the hurt, harm, and impact on our lives. God cares. Scripture includes clear descriptions of trauma, hurt, harm, and the damage done in people's lives. Some scriptures describing the impacts of hurt and harm are:

Psalm 34:18 A Promise
"The Lord is near to the brokenhearted and saves the crushed in spirit." (ESV)

Isaiah 61:1–2 A Declaration of Jesus
"The spirit of the Lord God is upon me, because the Lord has anointed me to bring good news to the poor; He has sent me to bind up the brokenhearted, to proclaim liberty to the captives, and the opening of the prison to those who are bound." (ESV)

Jesus chose this to announce His public ministry. The "healing of the broken hearted" is clearly top on His list of priorities!

- The word broken refers to breaking an item— a cracker, or a stick broken in two.

- It also refers to shattering— like a glass or piece of porcelain dropped and shattered into many pieces.

- Finally, it describes something crushed— like herbs crushed with a mortar and pestle, or grain crushed under a stone.

2 Peter 2:19 An Explanation
"For by whatever a person is overcome, they are enslaved." (ESV)

This verse is a side comment within a larger discussion of false teachers and people being deceived and dragged back into sin by others who love their sin, who "love to make money by doing evil." Peter is basically saying, "What overcomes [masters, takes control over] someone enslaves them."

What overcomes us? Our own sin, certainly. We can also be overcome by hurt and harm. What hurts and harms us has great influence, and that influence can be so powerful that we feel powerless, enslaved, or controlled. Often, freeing ourselves from the impact of that hurt and harm is very difficult. The hurt and harm themselves get in the way.

> Romans 7:15 An Example
> "For I do not understand my own actions. For I do not do what I want, but I do the very thing I hate." (ESV)

Paul lets us see his real struggle with old patterns of behavior: sin, error, old ways of mistreating others or wielding power and privilege. He says, "What I want to do I don't do … and what I don't want to do, I do! I am wretched!"

This dynamic is an impact of brokenness, a result of broken-heartedness. Sometimes, "What I want to do, I don't do" can refer to sin. Other times, it can refer to efforts to change old ways of thinking, acting, feeling, or speaking.

> James 1: 5-8 An Important Insight
> "If any of you lacks wisdom, ask God, who gives generously to all without reproach, and it will be given to you. But, ask in faith, with no doubting, for the one who doubts is like a wave of the sea that is driven and tossed by the wind. For that person must not suppose they will receive anything from the Lord; this is a double-minded person, unstable in all their ways." (ESV)

Let's focus on the phrase, "a double-minded person, unstable in all their ways." The writer describes this person as …"tossed about like something driven by the wind or the waves." He also says this person should not expect they will receive from God.

Note: "they will receive" is a description of ability to receive, NOT of God's willingness to give. The Greek word *lempsetai* means "to take hold of aggressively or strongly; to receive or take."

"Won't receive" gives an entirely different meaning than "to take hold of." Refusing to give anything because a person is doubtful, wavering, and uncertain is inconsistent with the always inviting, always seeking us before we seek Him nature of God. A literal rendition of this verse is: "they shouldn't expect they will [be able to] take hold of anything from God."

A friend once said, "I was really hurt. My whole life fell apart. God was giving to me and loving me, but I was like a radio with a broken receiver." The image of a hurt and hurting person with a "broken receiver" explains the dynamic of being unable to "take hold" of what God desires to give.

In addition, the word translated "double-minded" is a regrettable translation, because the Greek word is *di-psuchos,* meaning "two-souled." Common teaching about this is "if you are uncertain or doubting, you will be unstable and tossed around. And don't expect that God will give you anything in that doubting state!"

I suggest a much different reading: "If you are hurt and harmed so even your soul (your mind, will, and emotions— your identity) is broken, the result will be instability. You will be tossed around. You won't be able to receive the good God so wants to give you."

So the impact of hurt and harm can be brokenness (loss, damage) to our very souls, our identity and sense of who God made us to be, our thinking, our emotions, our decisions, and our choices.

Paul's painful crying out that he can't seem to do what his heart really intends, and instead does what he abhors, is a result of *di-psuchos,* two-souled-ness. Was Paul hurt and harmed in his life so that he lost himself? Was his soul wounded and damaged?

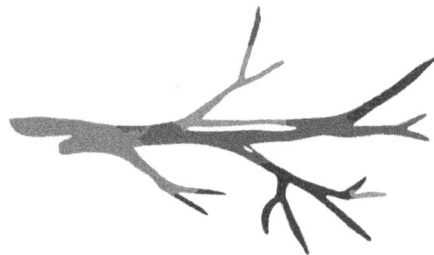

Please complete the Reflection Questions in preparation for Session TWO.

Please use this space for your reflections and responses.

REFLECTION QUESTIONS FOR THINKING AND JOURNALING

This week, please take time to think, feel, reflect, and write. Read each scripture in the previous section.

- Where do you see yourself in each scripture?

Recall an experience where you were hurt and harmed, and where you see impacts and effects in your life. Write in your journal:

- How do I see these scriptures (any, all, or none) reflected in this experience?

- Do I see the effects of *di-psuchos* in my life? (brokenness of the soul: in my heart, spirit, identity, thinking, emotions, will, or decisions)

- What do those effects look like?

- What happens in me when hurt and harm have broken my heart?

- How do I feel about that?

Last week, you asked God to shine a light on a specific experience or incident where you were hurt and harmed. Remembering that experience (or another if you prefer):

- How did that experience create brokenness in you?

- What does that look like?

- When you remember that experience, how do you feel?

- How does that experience get in the way of your growth, relationships, confidence, courage, or joy?

- What would you like to understand better?

DAILY IMMANUEL RHYTHM

To practice connecting with God in this way, please try a daily "Immanuel moment."

Here are the simple steps:

1. Pause. Reflect on what's going on and how you feel.

2. Breathe. Relax.

3. Ask God, Jesus, or Holy Spirit, "Please remind me of a time when I felt peaceful and happy."

  • God remembers. No hurry. Let Holy Spirit remind you. Sit with that memory for a moment. Feel the peace and the joy.

4. Ask God, Jesus, or Holy Spirit, "Where were you then?"

  • God WAS there. We are promised, "I am with you always," and, "I will never leave you." That means in the past, present, and future. The sure promise of God never changes. Just rest with God in that moment. Feel Him near. No hurry.

5. Ask God, "Where are you now?"

  • You may sense a picture. A memory. A physical sensation of peace or safety. A Scripture.

  • There is no right or wrong experience.

  • Just rest. Sit with God for a moment. No hurry.

6. Ask God, "What do you want me to know right now?"

- Listen. Sometimes people just keep sensing the closeness of God— and that is absolutely enough!

- God wants to connect with us, to speak to our hearts and into our lives, even more than we want Him to do it!

- God's ability to connect and speak to us is greater than our ability to "get it wrong."

7. At any point, you can return to the first Immanuel Moment: a time when you felt peace and joy. Any time, now or during your day, you can return to that moment. Because it isn't imagination— it's real. And God was there. And is there. And will meet us there. Enjoy.

END of preparation for Session TWO.
Group Session begins on the following page.

Please use this space for your reflections and responses.

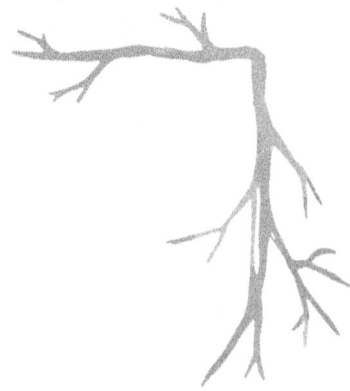

WATCH VIDEO

Please watch:
Session TWO
Broken Hearts, Broken Parts
at soulmending.live

BREAKOUT GROUP QUESTIONS

Facilitator reads: Welcome to our breakout group. Thank you for being here. A reminder of our Group Guidelines:

Confidentiality. What is said in this group stays in this group.

Protect privacy. In sharing, please don't give information that might identify someone who could be known by members of your group.

No cross-talk. Fixing, advice-giving, or offering solutions are not part of this group process. Instead of giving advice, you can say things like:

- "Thank you for sharing that."

- "Your insight really helped me."

- "I appreciate your [honesty, vulnerability, openness]. Thank you."

- "I'm learning from your insights."

Remember, your group gets to decide how you want to answer questions. You can choose one question to answer and focus on that. Each person can choose their own question. You can create your own questions and not choose any of these.

1. Psalm 34 and Isaiah 61 both refer to "broken hearts." James 1:8 refers to "broken parts."

Please use this space for your reflections and responses.

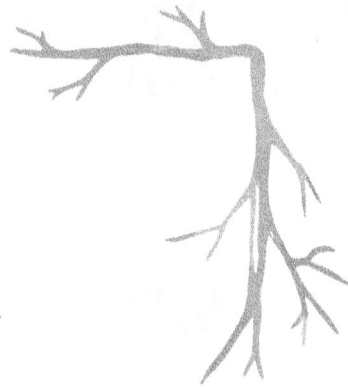

When you think of your life, have you experienced a "broken heart?"

- What happened?

- What did the "broken heart" look like?

- What did the "broken heart" feel like?

Have you experienced "broken parts?"

- Where do you see "broken parts" in your life?

  - broken thinking

  - broken choice-making

  - broken emotions

  - broken identity

2. When you think about your heart being "broken," what do you think? How do you feel?

3. When you think about your soul being "broken," what do you think? How do you feel?

4. In James 1:8, it says that *di-psuchos* people (people with broken souls) are unstable and "tossed around by every wave." It also says such people will not receive (take hold of good things) from God.

In the written summary and in last week's teaching, you heard that the phrase "such people will not receive from God" does NOT mean God refuses to give good things or take care of broken people. Instead, it means that someone hurt and harmed— so hurt that even their SOUL is broken— might not be ABLE to receive from God. God wants to give,and does give good and loving things. But the person is so hurt and harmed that they have trouble receiving those good things.

- Have you ever felt unable to receive good from God? OR

- Have you ever felt unable to receive good from other people? OR

- Have you ever believed you didn't deserve good things?

- What do you think about that now that you understand broken souls?

Please use this space for your reflections and responses.

LARGE GROUP

After breakout sessions, return to the large group. Spend 10 minutes sharing valuable insights from the Breakout Group.

WATCH VIDEO

Please watch:
Session TWO
Broken Hearts, Broken Parts
Conclusion
at soulmending.live

A fifteen-minute teaching wrapping up this session and introducing next week's topic.

Facilitator ends Session TWO with any announcements.

Please use this space for your reflections and responses.

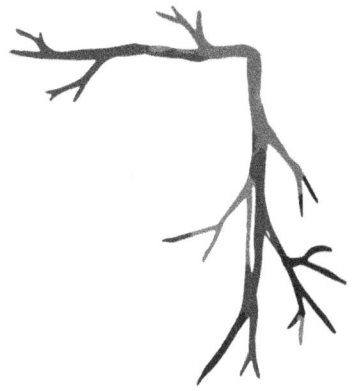

SESSION THREE

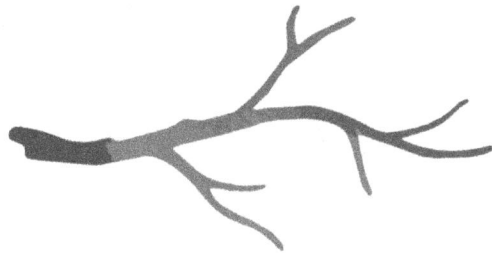

TRUTH, LIES, AND AGREEMENT

In the week between Sessions TWO and THREE, read the following and respond to the Reflection Questions for Thinking and Journaling.

Participants may also want to review the Breakout Group suggestions prior to participating in Session THREE.

Session Three
Truth, Lies, and Agreement

When we are hurt and harmed, we are wounded. This wound affects our identity and sense of self. It may affect our thinking, emotions, and decision-making. The enemy plants the seed of a lie in the wound. If the wound doesn't heal, we protect ourselves, and we feel afraid or powerless. The immediate scar fades with time, but the wound itself— the inner impact of hurt and harm— remains.

The Enemy of Our Souls is the father of all lies. And sometimes, the lie we hear comes from people. Others may say, "It was your fault," or, "Move on. Why do you keep wallowing? That happened a long time ago."

Perhaps the person who hurt and harmed you continues to reinforce hurtful, rejecting words and actions. We hear, "You're not worthy of love." Or, "What kind of man/woman/Christian/leader ARE you? You can't even do _____ successfully." Or, "I told you not to do _____. But you wouldn't listen."

A lie can come to us through shame. A culture of shame. A church community where shame is used to control people. A family where shame is used to maintain parental power, instead of love being used to teach and support "bruised reeds" (Isaiah 42:3) as they heal.

What are lies? Lies could be received. Sometimes they are believed, as a way of understanding or making sense of hurt, harm, and pain. When a person's soul is broken, they often believe lies as a way to cope or try to make sense of hurt and harm.

We may hear and/or believe lies like: "What happened was your fault. No one believes you. You should have _____. Stupid, how could you not have realized _____. You lost your chance. Now you'll be alone forever. God has bigger problems than you. Move on. You failed again. You ARE a failure."

Lies come in so many forms. Many people hear gender-related lies. For example, women often believe they aren't attractive enough. Body shaming becomes a debilitating state of being. The late-maturing, awkward teenager believes the lie that she will never be pretty or good enough. The single woman gets the not-so-subtle message that she is a third wheel, or that her desire for children is somehow selfish or silly.

In Christian cultures, assertive, intelligent women, or those who are natural leaders can get the message, "You're not the kind of submissive woman God uses." Or, "You better dial it down a little if you ever expect to get married."

Men are often attacked in their masculinity. "You're not much of a man," they hear. Taunts in gym class about a late-bloomer's lack of muscles, height, or athletic ability take root in the wound of being mocked or not chosen for the team. Family members belittle, "What kind of man can't do _____." Or, "Maybe you should join the army, they'll make a man out of you."

In Christian cultures, quiet or gentle men can get the clear message, "You're not leadership material." Or, "If you're not a leader, you can't be a real man."

People who do not fit in traditional, binary images of male or female can be hurt, harmed, and wounded by rejection and judgment. People assume the right to tell them who they are, why they are, and what they should do about it. This rejection can be crushing to the soul and spirit.

So the cycle goes: We are hurt. Our soul— our thinking, decision-making, emotions and identity— is broken. In trying to make sense of that hurt and the resulting wounds and pain, we can think or believe lies. Sometimes, we believe irrational lies. But often, we believe a lie because it seems true, or it feels true.

In time, we not only believe that lie, but we live our lives in agreement with that lie.

What does agreement look like?

Johanna landed a job right out of college. Three months later, the business was bought by a bigger company and she lost her job.

Johanna's next job seemed perfect. She'd hoped to work for a law firm in preparation for law school. About six months in, the firm lost a big client and laid off many staff, including Johanna.

Johanna's third job was a disaster from the start. Her boss made critical and cruel remarks about women. Johanna's days were filled with long, dull hours of document assembly. She worked 12+ hour days. She was bright and insightful, so other attorneys in the office often asked for her help with complicated projects. But nothing seemed to please her boss.

After six months, her boss gave her a terrible review, claimed she was lazy and her work was unacceptable. He said she would never have a mind for the law. Johanna was fired.

Johanna was exhausted. She looked at every single project and assignment she'd done in the past 6 months, searching for examples of "unacceptable" or "lazy." "Am I really not smart enough to be a lawyer?" she wondered.

Three jobs lost. "I'm a failure," Johanna thought. "I'm not intelligent enough to be a lawyer." Johanna's best friend Kate, a successful attorney working in a big-name firm, said, "Ridiculous! You absolutely do have a mind for the law. That guy doesn't know what he's talking about."

But, everywhere she looked, Johanna saw failure. She felt ashamed. Her old confidence had disappeared. She told herself, "Kate loves me too much to see the truth."

When we are hurt and harmed, it is human nature to explain and make sense of those experiences. We figure it out, sometimes believing our conclusions or explanations must be true. Continued experience can reinforce those beliefs. We continue to believe and say yes, because our experience supports the belief, even if it actually makes no sense.

We might know, deep inside, that a belief isn't accurate or true— but it sure feels true. Our experience seems to support that belief at every turn. We may say, "I believe it because it feels true."

In time, what "feels" true becomes a way of choosing, thinking, and living. In the Old Testament, we're told two people can't walk together unless they agree on the direction (Amos 3:3).

Think about that: agreeing makes a big difference.

When we believe lies, we "walk with" them, letting the lie influence how we think and choose to act. We make decisions and life choices, and see ourselves, others, and God in light of that lie.

We live what we agree with. Our agreement becomes our map and can set our direction. Lie-based thinking becomes lie-based living.

"true" versus "True": Experience-Based Lies

Sometimes we believe a lie because it feels true. Our experience demonstrates it's true. To a child with learning disabilities, for example, it may feel true that, "I can't learn things. I'm not smart."

As a child, it might even have been "true" that they were unable to learn some academic material. But did that moment make the belief "I can't learn things, I'm not smart" actually TRUE?

God's Truth is, "You CAN learn things. You are not dumb. God has made you with unique abilities in art, or technology, or building. Your ability to learn will shine in the right places."

What do we do with lies? What do we do with old agreements?

In the following Reflection section, you can use an ABCD worksheet to deal with your own "Truth, Lies, and Agreements."

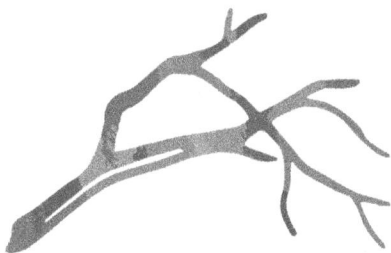

Please complete the Reflection Questions in preparation for Session THREE.

Please use this space for your reflections and responses.

Reflection Questions for Thinking and Journaling

Think of a time when you experienced hurt and harm. What happened?

How did you feel then? (If you need help identifying feelings, use the feeling lists on pg. 75 which appear under the heading: Four Basic Emotions.) You may list more than one emotion. If that happens, note the strongest emotion.

What did you think at the time?

As time passed, what did you come to believe:

- About yourself

- About other people

- About God

- About the world

If you don't know what you believed, ask God to show you. Pause. Listen. Simply ask, "God, what did I believe when that happened? Help me understand."

A reminder about listening to God: God speaks to us— we are His sheep who hear His voice and follow him, remember! He speaks in the ways we see in scripture, and they are many:

- An audible word

- Information

- An inner sense or experience

- The Truth of his character or nature

- Scripture

- A memory or something meaningful— even the lyrics of a song!

- The testimony of someone else

- Teaching, sermons, or books

Please use this space for your reflections and responses.

Reflecting on those beliefs, did any of them impact your life? Your decisions? Your relationships? Your confidence in or love for yourself? For others? Make a list.

Describe impacts here. What happened? What did these beliefs and their impacts cost you?

During Session ONE, you asked God to highlight an experience of hurt and harm that caused damage and loss in your life.

Ask God, "God, would you like me to understand more about this experience?"

If God says yes, spend some time completing the "Truth, Lies, and Agreement" section using the ABCD worksheet below, with that experience in mind.

If God says no, ask, "Do you want me to explore and understand more about another experience?"

If God says no, be at peace. Remember, this isn't a sprint to the finish line. It's a long, often slow journey into understanding, self-awareness, hearing God, and receiving healing and wholeness.

It took us a long time to get to where we are. And God will heal and change us at the pace that is right for us.

Use the ABCD Worksheet on the next page to reflect on your own "Truth, Lies, and Agreements."

Please use this space for your reflections and responses.

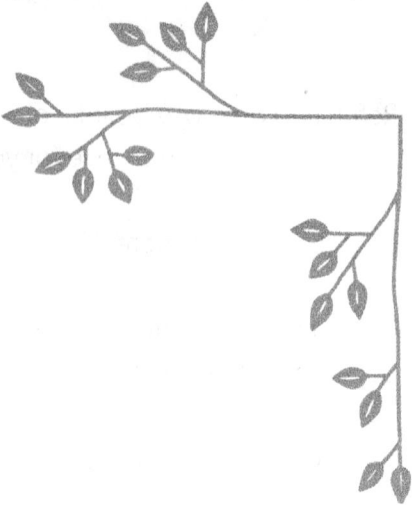

TRUTH, LIES, AND AGREEMENT ABCD WORKSHEET

What Happened?
I was hurt and harmed. What happened?

A: Ask God

- What did I believe?

- Is that True?

- What *is* True?

B: Break Agreement with the Lie

- I believed _____. That wasn't true. I agreed with a lie.
  No shame. No blame. We don't know what we know until we know it!

- I break agreement with the lie that _____.

C: Choose the Truth

- Jesus, you are the Truth.

- You showed me what was True. You said, _____.

- I choose to believe the Truth Jesus showed me:
  _____ (name that Truth).

D: Declare my true identity: Who does Jesus say I am?

- Jesus said _____ is true.

- That's true. So I am _____.
  Example: Jesus said He forgave me. Therefore, I am forgiven. I don't just get a little forgiveness— I *am* a forgiven child of God. I *am* forgiven.

Immanuel Prayer

Finally, if you find the Immanuel Prayer exercise meaningful, you may want to take time each day for an "Immanuel moment" with Jesus. Of course, if you feel more comfortable praying to God or Holy Spirit, that is absolutely fine!

Settle yourself.
Breathe.
Feel your body. Get comfortable.
Breathe in. Pause. Breathe out.
Relax.

1. Jesus, please remind me of a time when I felt happy and at peace.

- Listen.

- No hurry.

- Let yourself remember: Where were you? Any sounds or smells? What did you see? How did your body feel? What emotions arose?

- Let yourself enjoy this memory.

- Take a moment to appreciate Jesus— how kind and beautiful! He loved and cared for you in that time in memory. Just appreciate our beautiful Jesus!

2. Jesus, please show me where you were then.

- Pause.

- Listen.

- Rest with Jesus.

3. Jesus, please show me where you are now.

- Pause.

- Listen.

- Rest with Jesus.

4. Jesus, what do you want me to know today?

- Pause.

- Listen.

- Rest with Jesus.

5. Jesus, is there anything else you want me to know?

- Pause.

- Listen.

- Rest with Jesus.

Thank you, Jesus, for being with me.

- Take all the time you need to rest.

- Be still.

- Appreciate Jesus.

- No hurry. No worries.

- Peace.

END of preparation for Session THREE.
Group Session begins on the following pages.

Please use this space for your reflections and responses.

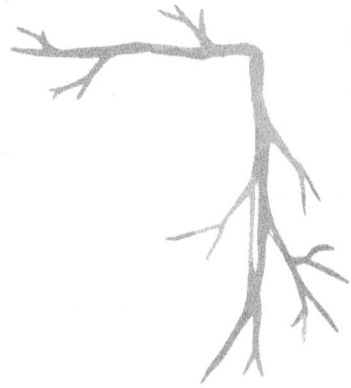

Watch Video

Please watch:
Session THREE
Truth, Lies, and Agreement
at soulmending.live

Breakout Group Questions

In preparation for this week, we have all been exploring, thinking and writing about "Truth, Lies, and Agreement."

Remembering that when we are hurt and harmed, we think and believe ideas to help us cope and survive. Sometimes we believe ideas because others have told us they are true. Sometimes we believe ideas because they seem to explain the hurt and harm that happened. Sometimes, what we believe seems to protect us from pain and shame.

And sometimes, what we believe just plain isn't true.

Here are some questions to choose from in your Breakout Group:

As you think about the hurt and harm you experienced, did you discover you have been believing anything that isn't true? What was the lie? Why do you think you believed it?

If you have believed lies in order to protect yourself or to manage painful feelings after you were hurt and harmed, how did believing those lies affect you? What were the results in your life? In your thinking? In your choices? In your relationships? In the way you see yourself? In your confidence and belief in yourself?

Have others ever expected or taught you to believe lies when you were hurt and harmed? How did that affect you? What do you think about it now?

- For example, some women who have experienced domestic violence are taught that they are responsible for the violence because they weren't submissive enough.

Did you try the ABCD tool to help you say no to lies and yes to Truth? What happened? What new ideas or insight did you discover when you used the ABCD tool?

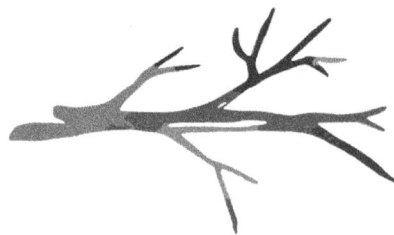

Large Group

After breakout sessions, return to the large group. Spend 10 minutes sharing valuable insights from the Breakout Group.

Watch Video

Please watch:
Session THREE
Truth, Lies, and Agreement
Conclusion
at soulmending.live

A fifteen-minute teaching wrapping up this session and introducing next week's topic.

Facilitator ends Session THREE with any announcements.

Please use this space for your reflections and responses.

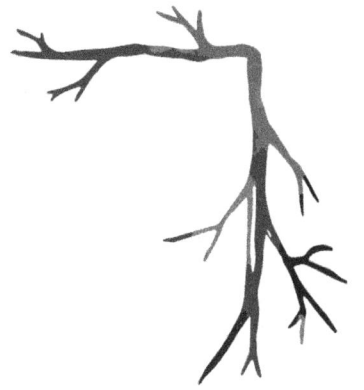

SESSION FOUR

FEEL AND DEAL: HEALING YOUR TRUE SELF

In the week between Sessions THREE and FOUR, read the following and respond to the Reflection Questions for Thinking and Journaling.

Participants may also want to review the Breakout Group suggestions prior to participating in Session FOUR.

BE REAL

What really happened?
What did the hurt and harm really cost me?
What were the real impacts in my life?
You are free to be honest.
No pressure to justify, excuse, or explain away.

FEEL

Permission to feel.
Freedom to feel.
The honest, deep emotions underneath the surface.
Permission to feel anger. Betrayal. Anguish. Grief. Fear.
No "bad" feelings or "good" feelings— just *your* feelings.

DEAL

It's a process.
No timeline or deadline.
Free to experience and understand …
emotions, experiences, thoughts, fears.
To count the cost of letting go.
To weigh the choices.
Free to reconcile.
Free to not.
Free to set boundaries.
Free to honor yourself and others.
Free.

HEAL

Take back your power.
Rediscover your dreams and desires.
Release yourself from wounds and lies.
Reclaim your strength as a courageous forgiver.
Return to your true self.

SESSION FOUR
FEEL AND DEAL:
HEALING YOUR TRUE SELF

Soul mending requires looking outside at what happened *to* us and inside at what happened *in* us.

Many of us grew up in families, churches, and cultures where we were taught to deny, minimize, excuse, or ignore both what happened *to* us and what happened in us as a result.

Many people are taught to dismiss or discredit what happened and the emotions they felt as a result. We tell ourselves things like, "Oh, it wasn't so bad. Other people had it much worse." Or, "I feel angry. Anger is not an emotion 'good people' feel."

Some people don't allow themselves to be real because they have been told that scriptures like, "Honor your parents," and, "Respect those in authority," mean they cannot tell or talk about what happened. They believe, "I was hurt by my parents (or a pastor, teacher, grandparent, someone in authority). If I talk about what happened, that wouldn't be honoring."

Many people of faith believe they must forgive, even when they aren't ready. They've been taught to pretend they weren't really hurt, to minimize harm. And often, people are taught that forgiving means reconciling with the person who hurt and harmed.

Jesus never minimized. He never pretended. Jesus was real. He was real when people did wrong things. He was real when people disobeyed God or hurt others, and He was also loving and so, so compassionate.

When He spoke to the woman facing the men with stones, He didn't say, "What you have done doesn't matter." He gently said, "I don't condemn you. Now go and don't live like this anymore."

When Thomas the disciple refused to believe Jesus was alive, even though Jesus Himself had told His friends He would be killed and return, Jesus didn't minimize Thomas's doubt. He honestly said, "Blessed are those who believe even when they have not seen," and He lovingly showed His wounded hands to Thomas. Jesus was willing to do whatever Thomas needed in order to believe. Imagine Jesus thinking, "Thomas, if that's what it takes for you to believe I am your Messiah, then go ahead— touch my wounds. See for yourself. I love you that much!" (John 20:24-29).

To find healing, it is necessary to be real. Because big hurt = big harm = big impacts, it is important not to pretend. Not to minimize or deny.

Jesus is not afraid of the bigness of our pain. He isn't surprised or disappointed when we feel big, painful emotions.

If our soul— our thinking, choosing, and emotions— is to be restored and made whole, it is important to be real about our thoughts, choices, and feelings.

So, when you come to Jesus, honestly sharing about what happened to you, it is just as important to be real about what happened in you— the emotions you felt then and feel now.

Included in this Session is a list of feelings. (See page 75.) "Big" feelings and small feelings. Strong feelings and not-so-strong feelings. For example, angry feelings come in many sizes and strengths. A small, not-so-strong angry feeling might be *frustrated* or *annoyed*. A BIG, strong, intense angry feeling might be *rage, furious,* or *exploding*.

Small feelings are okay. Big feelings are okay.

Feelings are not right or wrong— they just ARE. Feelings are signals, showing us what is happening *inside* us. Feelings give us information to help us understand what has happened and how we are being affected inside.

The Bible tells us to "be angry, but don't sin" (Ephesians 4:6). That means, *Yes, feel and experience anger. Feeling anger is not wrong. But, be aware, don't allow that anger to drive you to do sinful things.*

Often, emotions are like flashing lights, warning us, "Danger— someone is violating your boundaries," or, "Slow down— you're feeling overwhelmed because you're being pressured." We may feel uncomfortable because we're in danger. We might feel cautious or afraid because we're in the presence of someone who is not trustworthy.

Listen to emotions. Learn from them. Our emotions don't get to run the show. They give us information to help us decide what is wise and good. And we are in charge of what we do with those feelings.

Use the Four Basic Emotions list included with the Reflection Questions. In the past sessions, we asked God to remind us of a time we have been hurt and harmed. We've thought and written about the effects or impacts of those experiences. We've asked God to show us what we've believed and whether those beliefs are true.

This week, spend time being real and feeling the feelings experienced as a result of the hurt and harm.

Please complete the Reflection Questions in preparation for Session FOUR.

Please use this space for your reflections and responses.

Reflection Questions for Thinking and Journaling

Ask Jesus, "What hurt and harm would you like me to think about this week?"
Write a few sentences about what happened.

Be honest. Remember, Jesus never pretended. He was REAL, loving, compassionate and kind.
Please be REAL, loving, compassionate, and kind with yourself.

What happened?

What did I do?

What did the other person or group of people do?

How did I feel then? (Use the Four Basic Emotions list, found following this section.)

- What was my strongest feeling then?

- What other, smaller feelings did I experience?

- Describe the strongest feeling. Here are some ideas:
  Name the feeling. My strongest feeling was _____.

  My _____ feeling was like:

  - What color describes your feeling? (e.g. My angry feeling was bright red.)

  - Compare your feeling to something in nature. (e.g. My sad feeling was like a gray, foggy morning. Or, my afraid feeling was like a rabbit, shaking and unable to move.

  - Compare your feeling to a song, movie, or book. (e.g. My excited feeling was like the hobbits on the morning of Bilbo's great birthday party when they saw the wizard, Gandalf, come into the Shire with a wagon filled with fireworks!)

Please use this space for your reflections and responses.

- Compare your feeling with something in scripture. (e.g. My overwhelmed feeling is like when so many people wanted Jesus to help them that He finally had to get on the boat and go to the other side of the lake just to get a moment's peace!)

Use your Immanuel Prayer outline and bring that strong feeling to Jesus.

Tell Jesus what you felt when you were hurt and harmed.

Ask Jesus to show you where he was when you felt that difficult, painful feeling.

Ask Jesus, "What do you want me to know about my _____ feeling?"

- Listen

- Wait

- Give yourself all the time you need to hear Jesus, let his words soak into your soul, and think about what his words mean to you.

Ask Jesus, "Is there anything else you want me to know about my feelings about being hurt and harmed?"

- Again, listen.

- Wait— no hurry.

- Let his words soak into your soul. Think about what his words mean to you.

Look again at the Four Basic Emotions list (which follows these Reflection Questions). Think and write:

- What did I learn about feelings in my family growing up?

- What was life-giving and helpful? What wasn't?

- What feelings did my family allow?

- What feelings were NOT allowed?

- What do I think about that now?

- What feelings am I afraid to feel today?

- What do I do when feelings are "too big" or "too hard" or "not allowed?"

Please use this space for your reflections and responses.

Ask Jesus these questions, and write what he shows you below:

- "Jesus, what do YOU want me to do with my feelings?"

- "Jesus, how are my feelings part of my healing?"

- "Jesus, am I not being "real" in any way about what happened to me?"

- "Am I not being real in any way about what happened *in* me?"

- "Jesus, what do you want me to know now?"

FOUR BASIC EMOTIONS

HAPPY	SAD	ANGRY	AFRAID

HIGH Level Emotion Words

HAPPY	SAD	ANGRY	AFRAID
Elated	Miserable	Raging	Panicked
Ecstatic	Crushed	Furious	Horrified
Jubilant	Helpless	Outraged	Terrified
Overjoyed	Worthless	Hateful	Ashamed
Radiant	Depressed	Exploding	Desperate

MEDIUM Level Emotion Words

HAPPY	SAD	ANGRY	AFRAID
Delighted	Forlorn	Disgusted	Alarmed
Excited	Dejected	Irritated	Fearful
Bubbly	Alone	Hostile	Uncomfortable
Tickled	Defeated	Frustrated	Shaky
Glowing	Burdened	Upset	Jittery

LOW Level Emotion Words

HAPPY	SAD	ANGRY	AFRAID
Cheerful	Resigned	Grumpy	Uneasy
Glad	Down	Bothered	Tense
Pleased	Sad	Annoyed	Anxious
Amused	Gloomy	Confused	Nervous
Relieved	Ignored	Touchy	Puzzled

END of preparation for Session FOUR.
Group Session begins on the following page.

Please use this space for your reflections and responses.

Watch Video

Please watch:
Session FOUR
Feel and Deal: Healing Your True Self
at soulmending.live

Breakout Group Questions

Choose any, all, or none of these questions, as your group decides.

1. What do you think about the idea that feelings are neither right nor wrong?

2. What do you think about the idea that, in order to heal, we must be real about what happened?

   - What have you been taught about "being real?"
   - What has your experience been with trying to "be real?"

3. Did any insights or questions emerge from this week's reading and reflections?

4. What is most challenging for you about recognizing, exploring, and being real about your emotions/feelings?

Please use this space for your reflections and responses.

LARGE GROUP

After breakout sessions, return to the large group. Spend 10 minutes sharing valuable insights from the breakout group.

WATCH VIDEO

Please watch:
Session FOUR
Feel and Deal, Healing Your True Self
Conclusion
at soulmending.live

A fifteen-minute teaching wrapping up this session and introducing next week's topic.

Facilitator dismisses the large group with a blessing or prayer.

Please use this space for your reflections and responses.

SESSION FIVE

RESTORING THE SOUL

In the week between Sessions FOUR and FIVE, read the following and respond to the Reflection Questions for Thinking and Journaling.

Participants may also want to review the Breakout Group suggestions prior to participating in Session FIVE.

SESSION FIVE
RESTORING THE SOUL

This session is a time to step back and listen to our hearts. To rest. To take care of ourselves. It is a moment to take the hurt, harm, and impact we've recognized, and the grief and loss we've experienced, to Jesus. To feel the feelings. To be honest about what happened to us and in us.

And it's a time to put those thorny, difficult truths in Jesus' hands.

God is good. Everything He does is good. Everything in His will is good. If it isn't good, it isn't God. How could God be the source of evil? He isn't.

In 2 Peter 3:8, we learn that God is not slow to keep His promises. He is not ignoring evil or pain or need, but He is patient. His will is that everyone would turn from sin.

That's God's will.

In the same way, the hurt and harm that happened to us were not God's will. God NEVER said, "I will give this person cancer, or just let this person be sick or mentally ill or molested or harmed, so they will come closer to me." That's not how God is. God is love. God is good. Cancer and death, hurt and harm, assault and betrayal— all evil comes from Satan and from human sin. God is never the creator or giver of evil. It isn't possible because there is no darkness in Him, only light.

Free will is part of being human. God created humans with free will. What will God do with evil? He says He will redeem it. Transform it. Restore what is lost. Replace evil with good.

A principle in Scripture is that God returns to us what is stolen. In Proverbs 6:31, we're told a thief must repay seven times the amount stolen, and that Satan is a thief. The enemy in our battle is not flesh and blood, but powers, principalities, and evil in high places.

In Joel 2, God promises to "restore to you the years the locust has eaten." We're told God sees our grief and loss. He will transform mourning, grief, and sadness into celebration and dancing (Psalm 30). He will remove our mourning clothes and dress us in happiness.

These are promises of God. And each one recognizes and doesn't minimize very real loss. Real grief. Real sadness.

During the past sessions, we've been thinking, listening, writing, and reflecting about hurt and harm. About the real impacts, losses, and cost of wrongs done to us. This is hard and often painful work.

This session, we want to ask God to show us the promise of return. Of restoration. Of transforming mourning into happiness. To show us what this looks like in our lives, that what the enemy intended for evil, God will transform into good. That what was stolen from us will be returned.

Here are some reflection questions and practices for self-care.

Close your day:
Examen Prayer (as described below) or Immanuel Prayer.

Reflect:
What has been life-giving and joyful today?
Tell Jesus. What happened? How did you feel?

What has been difficult or challenging today?
Tell Jesus. What happened? How did you feel?

Jesus, this was my day (describe).

Jesus, please remind me of a time I felt happy.
Jesus, show me where you were.
Appreciate Jesus.

Jesus, please show me where you are right now?
Pause. Listen. No hurry.

Jesus, what do you want me to know about today?
Pause. Listen. No hurry.

Please complete the Reflection Questions in preparation for Session FIVE.

Please use this space for your reflections and responses.

REFLECTION QUESTIONS
FOR THINKING AND JOURNALING

You've now looked back at the hurt and harm that happened to you. The honest reality of what happened. What was done. What was said. What you experienced.

Write what you would like Jesus to know about the losses and cost you experienced.

An honest, real, human reaction to loss and cost is grief.
What is your grief like?

How does it feel when you experience that grief inside?

How would you describe it?

> In the book of Joel, God says, "I will restore to you the years the locust has eaten." (Joel 2:25)

> In Psalm 30, we read, "You [God] have turned my mourning and grief into celebration and dancing."

What might it look like to "restore to you the years the locust has eaten?"

Can you imagine your grief being transformed into happiness?

If your grief were transformed into happiness, what do you imagine it might look like?

Please use this space for your reflections and responses.

God promised to "restore" what His people have lost.

Ask God about your loss. Write anything God shows or speaks to you:

- God, when you see what the wrong, hurt, and harm I experienced has cost me, what do you want me to know?

- God, show me how you are restoring what I have lost.

- God, I haven't expected my losses to be restored. I haven't expected my grief to be transformed.

- And most importantly... Please forgive me for not believing you desired good for me. Please forgive me for not believing you would do good for me.

Please write any thoughts or feelings about this:

- God, is there anything else you want me to know about your promise to restore to me the years the locust has eaten?

This week, take time to rest.
Take time to do things you enjoy.
Take time to notice what is life-giving, what is easy and joyful, and what feels and seems good in your life.
Ask God to point out any way God is restoring what was lost:

Transforming pain
Doing good in your life
Making all things new
Making your broken parts whole
Restoring your soul

END of preparation for Session FIVE.
Group Session begins on the following page.

Please use this space for your reflections and responses.

Watch Video

Please watch:
Session FIVE
Restoring the Soul
at soulmending.live

Breakout Group Questions

The focus of this session is God's desire, will, and heart to restore what is broken in us. To replace lies with truth. To redeem what was stolen, and return us to wholeness and healing.

God doesn't want us to live with broken souls. He doesn't want us to have divided thoughts, scattered emotions, or confused, unclear decisions.

God wants us to be whole. He has promised to give back to us "the years the locust has eaten." And He shows us His heart when He says, "I will make all things new," or, "I will give you beauty in the place of ashes. The oil of joy instead of depression."

We also focused on recognizing and allowing ourselves to feel our real, honest feelings.

Here are some Breakout Group questions:

1. As I think about the hurt and harm I experienced, I realize the impact was _____.

   - I lost _____.

   - I know it was not God's will for me to be hurt and harmed.

   - What would it look like for God to restore what I lost?

   - How do I feel about that?

Please use this space for your reflections and responses.

2. Share any way you have experienced God restoring or returning what you have lost.

3. Were you taught that whatever happens must be God's will?

- Were you told that God "allows" bad things to happen because He wants you to come closer to Him?

- How did that affect you?

- What do you think about this now?

4. What important, new, or valuable insights (ideas, new ways of thinking, new ways of understanding) did you discover this week?

- How has that affected you?

Please use this space for your reflections and responses.

LARGE GROUP

After breakout sessions, return to the large group. Spend 10 minutes sharing valuable insights from the breakout group.

WATCH VIDEO

Please watch:
Session FIVE
Restoring Your Soul
Conclusion
at soulmending.live

A fifteen-minute teaching wrapping up this session and introducing next week's topic.

Facilitator dismisses the large group with a blessing or prayer.

Please use this space for your reflections and responses.

SESSION SIX

USING THE TOOLS: A PROCESS FOR HEALING

In the week between Sessions FIVE and SIX, read the following and respond to the Reflection Questions for Thinking and Journaling.

Participants may also want to review the Breakout Group suggestions prior to participating in Session SIX.

Session Six
Using the Tools:
A Process for Healing

When we are hurt and harmed, there is often a moment where we recognize the difference or "canyon of disconnect" between what we hoped would happen (wanted, needed, desired) and what *actually* happened.

We wanted or needed one thing, and received or experienced something very different. The space between the "want and need" and the "actual reality" is filled with hurt, pain, and loss. We feel emotions ranging from disappointment to devastating betrayal. In that space between hope and reality, we are harmed. The enemy lies to us, and we often believe those lies because, in our pain, they "feel" true. Then, the lies become patterns of thinking and doing, and the patterns shape our lives and identity.

In this session, we'll introduce a new tool called the "Incident Log." This outlines a process of exploring, reflecting on, and understanding what happened *to* us and *in* us.

Here is the outline of the Incident Log:

You experience something difficult, hurtful, or harmful. Ask yourself:

- What happened?

  - What did you do?

  - What did the other person/party do?

- What did you HOPE would happen? (desire, need, want, wish)

- What actually DID happen?

- How did you feel then?

  - How do you feel about this now?

- How were you affected by what happened?

- Who else was affected?

- What did you think or believe because of what happened?

  - How did those beliefs affect you and your life?

  - What was true?

  - What does Jesus want you to know about this?

- If you could do this over, what would you do differently?

- What do you wish the other person/party would do now?

- Finish with Immanuel Prayer, bringing this to Jesus.

This "Incident Log" is a tool to help us process, think about, and understand what happened *to* us and what happened *in* us.

This week, you will use this tool, the ABCD worksheet, and Immanuel Prayer to explore a specific experience of hurt and harm, and to bring that experience to Jesus for healing and restoration.

This is a time to listen to your body and spirit. To give yourself grace and space. No hurry. No rules.

You will write when you can, and only as much as you can.

Please give yourself time and grace as you think, reflect, and write this week. If you begin to feel "flooded" or overwhelmed, please stop. Rest. Talk with Jesus.

If you experience pain or emotions that feel unmanageable, please stop. Call a friend, your therapist, a pastoral person, or other trusted individual. You can end this session's writing at any time. Your emotional and physical safety are God's highest priority.

You may find it helpful to begin and end writing sessions with Immanuel Prayer. Just being in God's beautiful presence brings peace and helps us see more clearly.

Blessings on your writing.

Please complete the Reflection Questions in preparation for Session SIX.

Please use this space for your reflections and responses.

REFLECTION QUESTIONS FOR THINKING AND JOURNALING

In the past weeks, we have learned, thought, and talked about:

- How hurt and harm have damaging impacts in our lives.

- Being real by honestly recognizing what happened, how we were affected, and how we feel.

- The healing described in Scripture: to know Jesus came to heal, mend, and restore broken hearts; that sometimes hurt and harm actually damage our souls, and we live with broken souls.

- Lies we believe when we're hurt, and how to exchange those lies for Truth (ABCD).

- The Truth that God's will, intention, and heart is to restore us, to return what has been stolen, and that we can ask Jesus to "make all things new."

- How to understand more about our feelings so we can recognize, name, experience, and learn from them.

- Being REAL, FEEL, and DEAL by being honest about what happened, real about our feelings, and bringing our pain, hurt and broken thinking, decisions and feelings to Jesus.

- Receiving healing from Jesus— healing from pain, healing of identity, and healing of memories and grief.

This week, please ask Jesus, "What do you want to heal in my life now?"

When the Holy Spirit shows you, focus on that experience of hurt and harm as you engage in this process of soul mending.

Please use this space for your reflections and responses.

INCIDENT LOG

Write your thoughts or memories about the following:

1. What happened? Briefly describe the hurt and harm you experienced.

2. What did you do?

3. What did the other person or persons do?

4. What did you hope would happen?

5. What actually did happen?

6. How did you feel then?

7. How did the other person's (or persons') actions affect you? What damage, harm, or impact resulted?

8. Was anyone else affected? How? How do you feel about this?

9. What did you think or believe after you were harmed? How did your beliefs affect the way you lived? Your relationships? Ability to trust? Confidence? The way you saw yourself or treated yourself? The decisions you made? Other things?

10. Ask Jesus about what you believed. Was it true? What does He want you to know? If it helps, use the ABCD worksheet first introduced in Session THREE. It is included again at the end of this section.

11. What would you do differently now, if you could change what happened?

12. What do you wish the other person(s) would do now?

13. Immanuel Prayer— Bring yourself, your hurt and loss, your feelings, and your pain to Jesus, using the steps for Immanuel Prayer listed again at the end of this section. Remember, He came to mend broken hearts. He wants our souls to be whole— whole thinking, whole decisions, whole emotions.

14. Write any other thoughts, questions, feelings, or needs you are aware of— anything else you want Jesus to hear or know.

Please use this space for your reflections and responses.

ABCD WORKSHEET

A: Ask God

- What did I believe?

- Is that True?

- What IS True?

B: Break Agreement with the Lie

- I believed _____. That wasn't true. I agreed with a lie.
  No shame. No blame. We don't know what we know until we know it!

- I break agreement with the lie that _____.

C: Choose the Truth

- Jesus, you are the Truth.

- You showed me what was True. You said, _____.

- I choose to believe the Truth Jesus showed me:
  _____ (name that Truth).

D: Declare my true identity: Who does Jesus say I am?

- Jesus said _____ is true.

- That's true. So I am _____.
  Example: Jesus said He forgave me. Therefore, I am forgiven. I don't just get a
  little forgiveness— I *am* a forgiven child of God. I *am* forgiven.

IMMANUEL PRAYER

Settle yourself.
Breathe.
Feel your body. Get comfortable.
Breathe in. Pause. Breathe out.
Relax.

1. Jesus, please remind me of a time when I felt happy and at peace.

   - Listen.

   - No hurry.

   - Let yourself remember: Where were you? Any sounds or smells? What did you see? How did your body feel? What emotions?

   - Let yourself enjoy this memory.

   - Take a moment to appreciate Jesus— how kind and beautiful! He loved and cared for you in that time in memory. Just appreciate our beautiful Jesus!

2. Jesus, please show me where you were then.

   - Pause.

   - Listen.

   - Rest with Jesus.

3. Jesus, I've been trying to understand what happened to me. (In a few words, tell Jesus what happened and how you feel now.) I need you to heal my heart.

Please show me where you are now.

   - Pause.

   - Listen.

   - Rest with Jesus.

4. Jesus, what do you want me to know about what happened?

- Pause.

- Listen.

- Rest with Jesus.

5. Jesus, is there anything else you want me to do now?

- Pause.

- Listen.

- Rest with Jesus.

6. Jesus, is there anything else you want me to know?

- Pause.

- Listen.

- Rest with Jesus.

7. Take a moment to return to that time when you felt happy and at peace. Just appreciate Jesus there— how He loves and comes to meet you. His kind face. How much He loves you.

- Pause.

- Listen.

- Rest with Jesus.

You can return to steps 4, 5, and 6 in the Immanuel Prayer outline if you would like to bring anything else to Jesus.

END of preparation for Session SIX.
Group Session begins on the following page.

Please use this space for your reflections and responses.

WATCH VIDEO

Please watch:
Session SIX
Using the Tools: A Process for Healing
at soulmending.live

BREAKOUT GROUP QUESTIONS

1. What was it like for you to carefully take apart and examine your experiences, emotions, and impacts of a difficult event of hurt, harm, and loss?

2. Any insights or new understanding?

3. As you explored the "space" between what you hoped for and what actually happened, what were your emotions? What insight or new understanding occurred?

4. Has learning how to encounter Jesus with specific hurt and harm helped you? How?

Please use this space for your reflections and responses.

LARGE GROUP

After breakout sessions, return to the large group. Spend 10 minutes sharing valuable insights from the breakout group.

WATCH VIDEO

Please watch:
Session SIX
Using the Tools: A Process for Healing
Conclusion
at soulmending.live

A fifteen-minute teaching wrapping up this session and introducing next week's topic.

Facilitator dismisses the large group with a blessing or prayer.

Please use this space for your reflections and responses.

SESSION SEVEN

HEALING: MENDING OUR BROKEN SOULS

In the week between Sessions SIX and SEVEN, read the following and respond to the Reflection Questions for Thinking and Journaling.

Participants may also want to review the Breakout Group suggestions prior to participating in Session SEVEN.

SESSION SEVEN
HEALING:
MENDING OUR BROKEN SOULS

Kintsugi is a Japanese art. In ancient times, porcelain was a precious possession. When a cherished piece of porcelain broke, Japanese artists used molten gold to mend it. Whether it was a practical household item or a statue or work of art, they would use seams of gold to replace and restore broken pieces into a new, whole creation.

In much the same way, we bring our broken places— broken hearts, broken souls, broken thinking, broken decision-making, broken emotions, broken identity— to God for healing. God does not erase the hurt and harm. He doesn't magically make the scars and broken places disappear. Instead, He mends us with the precious gold of His love and grace. Forgiveness replaces pain. New creation replaces the lost self and the fear-driven, self-protective false identity.

God's mending "gold" can be replacing lies with Truth. It can be telling us who we really are by removing the false self of fear and lies and restoring our true self. God can also mend our broken souls by going with us to the past, showing us where He was and always will be when hurt and harm happened. He can and will speak truth and love right into the memories of hurt and harm— not changing reality, but showing us the Truth we couldn't see earlier because of pain and loss. Also, He shows us where Jesus was when we were hurt and allows us to experience His presence, love, and grace in the place of loneliness, betrayal, shame, and lies.

When our real experiences of hurt and harm are witnessed, our experience is validated. Jesus witnesses our pain and loss. He is the witness who says, "I see you and I care."

We are healed in the moment of His presence. We are healed and mended by His generous, unconditional, great love.

How do we come to God for healing?

We come to God for healing in different ways.

- Sometimes, we experience strong, painful, or difficult emotions.

We feel overwhelmed and sometimes confused. Sometimes we know where those emotions came from. We can say, "_____ happened, and I felt _____." At other times, we feel these strong, painful feelings and aren't sure why or where they came from. We just know we're in pain.

Laura had lived in an apartment for more than 20 years. It was a cozy, home-like place on a beautiful street. Then one day, her landlord told her and the other tenants the building had been sold. Soon, Laura received a notice that the owners were moving into her apartment and she had to leave.

Although Laura was a successful professional with a well-paying job, she suddenly was flooded with feelings of fear and panic. She began to have nightmares about being homeless. She felt helpless and unsafe.

"I have enough money and friends to help if I need a temporary place to stay," Laura told herself. But even so, she could not stop the waves of fear and panic. Laura was in pain, but she wasn't sure why. The pain was clear, but the real, deep reason beyond her current housing situation was not clear.

- Some people come to God for healing because of memories.

Maybe painful, frightening, disturbing memories have been bothering us for a long time. Perhaps they suddenly re-appeared and won't go away. Those difficult memories can interfere with daily life or intrude on our relationships.

Years ago, **Monica**'s mom was depressed and couldn't take care of Monica or her sister. Monica was terrified they wouldn't have money for food. When school started, she realized her feet had grown. Her shoes were too small. She didn't tell her mom, because she knew there was no money for shoes. She just wore the shoes, even though her feet hurt every day. And every day, she felt afraid and ashamed.

Last week, the temperature dropped and Monica pulled out her leather boots. When she closed the zipper, it broke. Monica thought about replacing the boots. Suddenly, memories crowded into her mind. Memories of her mom lying on the couch. Memories of putting on the too-small, painful shoes. Memories of walking to school day after day with blistered feet. Suddenly, Monica felt afraid and ashamed.

She didn't know what to do with such old memories. She tried to tell herself, "The past is passed, let go." But that didn't help.

- Some people come for healing because of a here-and-now crisis or traumatic events.

In Jay's family, privacy didn't exist. In their crowded house, no child had toys or clothes of their own. Four boys slept in a single bedroom in bunks. The whole family used the one bathroom. While Jay showered, one brother might be on the toilet while another brushed his teeth. Both mom and dad walked into any room at any time. Changing your clothes? Nobody cared. In the shower? Too bad.

Jay remembered feeling so angry as a kid. When he asked for privacy, his siblings and parents laughed at him. He didn't want anyone in the bathroom when he changed clothes or took a shower. Yet no one listened. Jay felt rising, constant anger.

Last week, Jay came to work to discover someone had rifled through his desk. His jacket was gone. A gift card in the drawer stolen, and a framed photo of Jay and his nieces lay broken on the floor. The thief even took the coffee mug that had been a gift from his sister last Christmas. Jay told himself, "None of this is worth much. I'm fine. Nobody was hurt."

But, Jay felt a rising panic. "Someone touched my stuff," he thought. "They touched the picture of me and the girls. THEY TOUCHED IT!"

Jay's panic gave way to anger. He clenched his fists, wishing he had something to hit or throw, or someone to yell at. "Leave me alone! This is MINE."

- At other times, people come to God for healing because of a current, negative, painful experience.

Rachel applied for a better job with her employer. She knew her experience and skills were exactly what the position required. "I can do this," she told herself. "I'm the best qualified applicant."

Rachel was asked to interview. She felt confident and well-prepared. After the interview, she felt even better. The interviewer said, "Your experience is exactly what this department needs. You'll hear from me by the end of the week."

But Friday came and went without a call. Rachel felt confused. She knew the other applicants and was certain she was the strongest. "I should get this job," she told herself.

On Monday, Rachel received a letter from Human Resources saying, "Thank you for your interest in this position. We regret to say another applicant was chosen and the position has been filled."

What? Rachel felt confused. Then she opened an email from her boss. "Rachel, I'm sorry you didn't get the job," it read. Her boss then included the name of the person who was hired. It was the department director's best friend!

Suddenly, Rachel felt so angry. She felt betrayed and unsafe. She didn't know what to do. Who could she trust?

- At other times, people come for healing because their thinking, emotions, decision-making and sense of who they are seems fragile and fragmented.

They can't think straight and aren't sure why. Their feelings pin-ball all over— high and low, strong and disappearing. Painful and numb. It's so confusing. Sometimes people realize they feel tossed around by anything and everything, like a piece of driftwood in wild waves, hurled into the air and crashing to shore. Out of control. Confused. Thinking, "I don't know who I am or what I want. I don't know how to manage myself or my life."

Clare grew up in a troubled family where her father raged and hit. Her mother hid and pretended. The children learned to be silent and scarce when dad was around, and to put on the masks of a smiling family around the dinner table when dad was gone, and mom was busy pretending to be the "good Christian family."

Clare and her siblings felt confused and afraid. They believed, "I am nobody. Nothing. To survive, I must do what mom and dad want."

As years went by and Clare became an adult, she learned to become whomever others wanted or needed her to be. Like a chameleon, she changed shape, form, and personality to please everyone. She felt what others allowed her to feel. She thought and made decisions to keep others happy. She truly had no idea who she was. Shopping for clothes was a torture. She had no idea whether she even liked that outfit, let alone whether it looked good on her. Goals seemed impossible. How could she dream and make plans if she didn't know which part of her would show up at any given moment?

How does Immanuel Prayer help us heal?

In order for hurt and harm to become healing and wholeness, we must recognize (be real), understand (feel and deal), and discover our true selves in the midst of the trauma and loss.

And, part of this process is witnessing— seeing and recognizing— what happened.

Laura, Monica, Jay, Rachel, and Clare struggled to witness their own experiences, because the hurt and harm was so big and painful. What they believed in order to survive was so confusing. Even if they knew their thoughts and beliefs weren't true, they felt true. All five struggled to answer the question, "Who am I? What is unique and valuable about me? When am I being my true, joyful, honest self?"

Immanuel Prayer helps us heal because we can bring the hurt, harm, pain, confusion, and loss of identity to Jesus Himself. And Jesus will witness what happened. He will speak truth in the place of fear-driven, survival-based lies. He will see who we truly are, and love, honor, and validate that self.

Jesus is our witness.

Jesus hears and sees.

How to Come to God for Healing

As mentioned in the stories above, we come to God with pain and hurt in many forms.

- When bringing **a here-and-now experience** to Jesus for healing— we have been hurt and harmed, and are having a hard time moving on or returning to a place of peace— we can honestly (without minimizing or excusing) tell Him what happened. See the outline below for detailed suggestions about how to bring a here-and-now experience to Jesus for healing.

- When we experience **a recurring, painful emotion**, a helpful prayer approach is to be honest about your real feelings. Notice when and how painful emotions show up. Ask God to show you any lies you believe or any past trauma linked to a particular painful emotion. See the outline below for detailed suggestions about bringing painful emotions to God.

- When **a specific memory** from the past has left us tangled and caught in pain and hurt, the memory may return, perhaps like a film being rewound and replayed day after day. Or, whenever a similar experience happens, that old memory rushes to the surface. Perhaps we have forgiven, sometimes repeatedly, yet the memory persists. Perhaps we have tried to understand and find God's goodness in and in spite of that memory. But regardless, the memory continues to hinder our happiness, peace, and joy.

  But coming to God with painful, specific memories is another way we find healing. Ask Jesus, God, or Holy Spirit to accompany you and take you back to the memory, remembering that time has no beginning or end for God. He is and was and will always be in all times. He promised He would always be with us, which means He was with us in the past and will be with us in the present and future. With God, Jesus, or Holy Spirit, return to the experience when that painful memory occurred. You have asked Him to be with you. You can trust that He will be.

  Note: With very painful, traumatic memories, it is wise to do this only with a trusted friend or prayer minister.

Here are the paragraphs above in an outline form. You can use this to guide your prayer time.

Outlines: Tools for Bringing our Souls to God for Healing

Current, Here-and-Now Experience

- Tell Jesus what happened — honest and real.

  - How did you feel?

  - How were you affected? Ask Jesus to show you any other impacts on you or your life.

- Tell Jesus what you thought. Ask Jesus, "Did I believe any lies because of what happened?"

  - Use the ABCD tool

- Immanuel Prayer

Painful Emotion

- Tell Jesus what you feel. Be real. He is not afraid of our emotions. Remember, emotions are not right or wrong— they just are. They give us information about ourselves and others. (Use the Four Basic Emotions List, if that helps.)

- Ask Holy Spirit, "What are the roots of this emotion? What happened? What does Jesus want me to know about this?"

  - What beliefs are connected with this emotion? Am I believing any lies? (Use the ABCD Worksheet.)

  - See the tools for Memories below, and ask Jesus to remind you of any memory that is a root of that painful emotion.

Painful Memory or Memories

- Ask Jesus, God, or Holy Spirit to accompany you back to that memory.

- Look for Jesus. Ask, "Jesus, where are you?"

- Let yourself feel what it's like to be back in that memory. If you need Jesus to be closer to you, just ask. You can hold on tight to Jesus, no matter where you are.

- Knowing Jesus was present and cares about what happened is one way to reject the lies of the enemy and hear and receive the Truth Jesus wants us to know.

- Ask Jesus, "What do you want me to know about this?

  - No hurry.

  - God is always speaking and showing love to us. Always. We recognize His presence and voice in different ways, such as:

    - Images— a picture or sometimes a "video"

    - Memories of God showing up

    - Emotions, or sensing His love or presence

    - Scripture and/or Truth we know is from God

    - Memories of meaningful experiences— sometimes places, nature, books, words, or songs

    - Seeing or hearing Jesus with our ears and eyes, or with our spirits "sensing" His presence and love

- Ask Jesus, "What did I believe because of what happened to me? What is the Truth about what happened?"

  - Use the ABCD Worksheet

Remember, we are here to accompany one another into the presence of Jesus. To the heart and throne of God. To hear and be transformed by the voice of Holy Spirit.

We don't have to solve, fix, or give advice. Immanuel means "God with us" for a reason! What a beautiful, sacred space. What a privilege to accompany each other to Jesus for healing.

Memories and Tools

The teaching in the previous session (Session SIX) focused on a brief review of tools, such as the ABCD acronym, to help explore, understand, identify, and break agreement with lies we've believed. Also, how to hear from God and choose not only the Truth in place of those lies, but also the identity those lies stole and compromised in us.

In addition, information was shared describing how Holy Spirit heals specific, painful memories by returning to them with us. Remembering this is not imagination or changing the truth of what happened, it is God re-entering past pain and loss. It is God showing us where He was when we were hurt. It is God showing us how He saw what happened then and sees what is still happening in us now.

Finally, we ended with encouragement to make the tools of *Soul Mending* part of our regular lives and spiritual practices. With the principles of:

- **Be Real.** Honestly recognize hurt, harm, and impacts.

- **Feel.** Honestly recognizing, naming, and experiencing emotions--both when we experienced hurt and harm in the past, and currently in the here and now. Ask God for help discerning where the thoughts, beliefs, emotions, fears, and doubts in our minds are actually coming from— from God, the Enemy, Other People, or our own Broken Soul.

- **Deal.** Deal with the hurt, harm, and impacts by asking God to show us the lies we believed when we were hurt. The lies we believed when harm led to impacts that stole identity, value, trust, and capacity for healthy relationships. To deal also means to seek God about what is true and what replaces lies. (ABCD).

- Last, we **Heal.** God shows us Truth. We break agreement with lies and discover new ways to see ourselves, God, others, and the world through a lens of Truth instead of pain-driven lies. We heal as we ask God to show us our true identity, and as we embrace that identity. Believe it. Declare it to be true. And begin to live it.

Finally, this *Soul Mending* workshop ends with strong encouragement to make Immanuel Prayer a daily spiritual practice and a go-to means of self-care and engaging one's soul with God when hurt and harm occur in our lives.

The graphics and details for ABCD and Immanuel Prayer were included in previous sessions' summary and teaching materials. All group participants were encouraged to practice these healing tools.

Please use this space for your reflections and responses.

REFLECTIONS

Take time to re-read these pages of teaching and information. Note your thoughts, ideas, and questions.

Make copies of tools:

- ABCD
- Immanuel Prayer
- Emotions List
- Incident Log

You may want to meet as a group or with another person and try out the steps outlined above in the outlines for:

- A current, difficult experience
- A strong emotion
- A memory of past hurt, harm, and impact

End with Immanuel Prayer, returning to that place and time where Jesus was there and you felt safe and at peace.

Ending prayer sessions with an Immanuel Prayer encounter is important. It returns us to our place of safety and wholeness— in the presence of God, listening for His loving, kind voice, and feeling the reality of His always-with-you care.

END of preparation for Session SEVEN.
Group Session begins on the following page.

Please use this space for your reflections and responses.

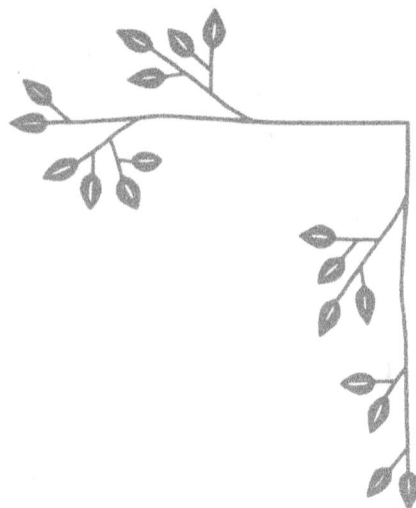

WATCH VIDEO

Please watch:
Session SEVEN
Healing: Mending Our Broken Souls
at soulmending.live

BREAKOUT GROUP QUESTIONS

Use this final Breakout Group to share any insights, new thoughts or ideas, or questions from the material in this final session— the text or video— or from previous sessions.

Please use this space for your reflections and responses.

LARGE GROUP

After breakout sessions, return to the large group. It's time to celebrate! Spend 10 minutes sharing valuable insights about what is "being made new" during the time you've been together in this workshop.

WATCH VIDEO

Please watch:
Session SEVEN
Healing: Mending Our Broken Souls
Course Conclusion
at soulmending.live

This video contains Julia leading the group through Immanuel Prayer, followed by a Blessing.

Facilitator dismisses the large group with a final blessing or prayer.

Please use this space for your reflections and responses.

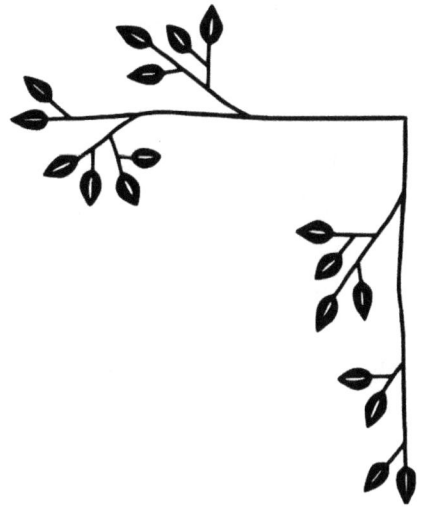

ACKNOWLEDGEMENTS

To my three incredible daughters and their spouses— Beth and Casey, Becky and Alex, and Ruth and Michael— I am deeply grateful for your determination to see *Soul Mending* become a reality. Special thanks to my son-in-law, Michael, for "project managing" and the beautiful design. This is for all of you.

To my partners in ministry at Youth With A Mission (YWAM) and Because Justice Matters (BJM), who opened my heart to women who have suffered trauma and opened doors of opportunity for me to put these *Soul Mending* sessions into practice. Thank you from the bottom of my heart to Allison, Lydia, Sonya, Sylvia, Lauren, Emily, Gabby and Mateo, Justine and Jason, Ruthie, Tim and Karol, Steve and Kayla, Josh and Kassie, and Malia and David for believing in me and always being there with your wisdom and support.

Heartfelt thanks to Dr. Karl Lehman for his insight and wisdom about Immanuel Prayer. It has been life-giving to me and so many others.

To my forever friends, Dave and Neta Jackson, as well as Tom and Lorita Boyle, Kelsey and Annie Evergreen, MaryBeth Haunty, Mary Ann Hunt, Kelley Scott, Craig and Tina Wong, Pastor Sharon Huey, and Nina McLawhorn— we know how to talk our heads off, don't we, about writing and ideas and just "stuff." Have we solved the world's problems yet? Probably not. But we tried! Thanks for believing in *Soul Mending* and going the extra mile to help it become a reality. All the laughter in the midst of everything has been helpful too!

Last but never least, deepest love and appreciation to my Circle Group of sisters: Irene Fong, Karen Seth, Kim Towsley, Margie Chiang, and Tina Wong. You have been with me in prayer and presence through many hard times as well as celebrations of everyday joy! I love you all.

RESOURCES

immanuelapproach.com
>Dr. Karl Lehman
>Immanuel Approach Basic Training Series: Online course, 10 DVD video series.

immanuelpracticum.com
>Pastor Patti Velotta
>eBook: see Get A Copy Quick
>Order: 847.247.4350

immanuelpractice.com
Soul Free: An Honest, Self Honoring Process of Forgiving
>A workbook-based approach to healthy practice of forgiveness.
>Julia Pferdehirt
>soulmending.live
>infosoulmending@gmail.com

Boundaries and Trust in Relationships
>A workbook-based approach to boundary-setting in relationships.
>Julia Pferdehirt
>soulmending.live
>infosoulmending@gmail.com

ABOUT JULIA PFERDEHIRT

Julia Pferdehirt is an author, educator, and professional storyteller. A Midwesterner by birth, she grew up in Parchment, Michigan. After graduating from university, she raised her family in Evanston, Illinois, and Madison, Wisconsin, while writing books, doing pastoral work and teaching.

After moving to San Francisco in 2013, Pferdehirt began to follow her passion, working with women seeking healing and change, including survivors of abuse and domestic violence. She developed the material which became this *Soul Mending* workbook by leading workshops hosted by a local church, at unconventional venues such as Burning Man, and as a versatile training tool with a small group of women known as the Circle Group.

Julia Pferdehirt is also the Director of Healing and Women's Ministry with "Because Justice Matters," an extension of YWAM (Youth with a Mission) San Francisco. As a licensed psychotherapist and pastor, she has worked with homeless, exploited, and marginalized women in the Tenderloin neighborhood of San Francisco. "Because Justice Matters" builds relationships to connect women with hope, recovery, emotional and spiritual healing, and each other.

But if you ask her to tell you about herself, Julia will laugh and say, "I'm the proud mother of three incredible, talented daughters, and grandmother of five amazing granddaughters— Maxime, Blair, Michael, Mabel, and Goldie!"

Books Written by Julia Pferdehirt

Blue Jenkins: Working for Workers by Julia Pferdehirt. Wisconsin Historical Society Press, October 2011.

Unwrap the Gifts: Receive Your Spiritual Inheritance Through Prayer Ministry by Paul Cox with Julia Pferdehirt. Creation House Publisher, July 2008.

Caroline Quarlls and the Underground Railroad (Badger Biographies Series) by Julia Pferdehirt. Wisconsin Historical Society Press, March 2008.

More Than Petticoats: Remarkable Michigan Women (More than Petticoats Series) by Julia Pferdehirt. Two Dot Books, June 2007.

Wisconsin Forest Tales by Julia Pferdehirt. Trails Custom Publishing, January 2004.

They Came to Wisconsin (New Badger History Series) by Julia Pferdehirt. Wisconsin Historical Society Press, October 2002.

Eight Curriculum Guides for the TRAILBLAZER series by Julia Pferdehirt with Dave and Neta Jackson. Bethany House Publishers, January 2000.

Freedom Train North: Stories of the Underground Railroad in Wisconsin by Julia Pferdehirt. Living History Press, January 1999.